Always Kiss Me Goodnight

by Deborah "Dee Dee" Dickson
Illustrated by Ronan Dickson

Copyright © Always Kiss Me Goodnight, 2024
www.neversaygoodbye.ca
Ontario, Canada

All rights reserved. Without limiting the rights under copyright reserved above, no part of this publication may be reproduced, stored in, or introduced into a retrieval system, or transmitted in any form or by any means (electronic, mechanical, including photocopying, recording or otherwise), without the prior written permission of the copyright owner of this book.

This publication contains the opinions and ideas of its author and is designed to provide useful information in regard to the subject matter covered. The author is not engaged in professional services in this publication. This publication is not intended to provide a basis for action in particular circumstances without consideration by a competent professional. The author expressly disclaims any responsibility for any liability, loss, or risk, personal or otherwise, which is incurred as a consequence, directly or indirectly, of the use and application of any of the contents of this book. While the author has made every effort to provide accurate information at publication time, the author assumes no responsibility for author or third-party websites or their content.

Deborah Dickson and Ronan Dickson
Always Kiss Me Goodnight
Includes bibliographical references.

Paperback ISBN 978-1-7388927-0-9
eBook ISBN 978-1-7388927-3-0
Audiobook ISBN 978-1-7388927-1-6

Growing Up & Facts of Life | Difficult Discussions | Death & Dying
Growing Up & Facts of Life | Family Life | Parents
Growing Up & Facts of Life | Friendship, Social Skills, & School Life | Emotions & Feelings

Chronic Illness | Single Parent | Angel | Heaven | Afterlife | Funeral | Trauma

This book is sold subject to the condition that it shall not, by way of trade or otherwise, be lent, re-sold, hired out, or otherwise circulated without the author's prior consent in any form of binding or cover other than that in which it is published and without a similar condition including this condition being imposed on the subsequent purchase.

I dedicate this book to my Mom, Wanda Marie.

Born: January 24, 1936
Died: November 8th, 1974

She was the light of my life...my world.
May our souls always be together.

When I was young, my mommy would tuck me into bed every night. We would say a prayer, exchange a kiss, and then the lights went out.

Some nights when I was upset, she would say, "You have to be strong. There will be difficult times in your life, and you will need to use the strength you have inside to face them. Remember these words, 'I am strong – I can do this' and keep telling yourself that whenever you find yourself facing challenges, big or small." Most nights, we would say the usual prayer together.

"Now I lay me down to sleep, I pray the Lord my soul to keep, Angels watch me through the night, 'til I awake in the morning light."

She kissed me every night. Daddy would kiss me too. I went to sleep feeling loved and safe. Family was everything.

When we built a house on our grandparent's farm, it brought our family even closer together. We had new routines, new chores, and new memories. I loved the fresh air. Country living felt so much better than living in the city. Living on a 100-acre farm, we felt connected with nature. We looked after farm animals, ran around the barn, rode the wagon and tractor, planted gardens, worked in the field bailing hay or straw, played with our pets, and enjoyed our new family adventures.

Our grandmother baked such delicious meals and desserts. Our grandfather introduced us to watching hockey, playing cards, fishing, and picking berries. For Sunday dinner, we were either at their house or ours. The new family traditions were important. So were rules and manners, for both our grandparents and parents. They taught us when to say 'please' and 'thank you', when to wait your turn, when to help others, and when to show respect.

We knew there was always abundant love around us. Our grandparents' farm provided so much fun. We had lots of laughs, lots of work, lots of family times and memories, but there were also some heartaches too.

One morning Mommy said, "Olivia, Bobby, today is the day! Grab your hats and strawberry baskets from the garage. As Grandma says, 'don't dilly-dally, let's get going.' Remember your manners. Help Grandma into the car. We are all going strawberry picking. Since we all love Grandma's strawberry jam, we need to pick lots of strawberries. If we all pick together, it won't take long. And remember, I know you love strawberries, but we need some to go in our baskets too!" We all laughed.

"Come on Bobby," I called. "Hurry up! Grandma is waiting for us in the car! Don't dilly-dally Bobby! We have to race to the patch and start picking!"

We loved picking berries with Grandma and helping her make jam. Of course, we had to sample them as we went! If we did a good job, she would sometimes give us money for our piggy banks.

"Don't eat too many berries, Kit," Grandpa said. Kit was his pet name for me. We didn't. There were about 20 jars of strawberry jam made that day.

"Grandma, we love you. Thank you for coming with us and making the jam!"

Another time Mommy said, "Olivia and Bobby, please pack your backpacks...it's vacation time! We are going camping! It is time for family fun! We will have hot dogs, campfires, toast marshmallows, go on walks, and sing campfire songs. We know you love sleeping in a tent, going fishing, swimming, and hiking. Are you excited?"

"Daddy and Mommy, we can't wait!" I replied. "We will pack right away!"

"Make sure you bring sunscreen, toothbrushes and toothpaste, jackets, water bottles, bug spray, pillows, and sleeping bags. It is going to be so much fun!" Mommy said.

"Can I bring my favourite teddy bear and doll too?" I asked. "Bobby, remember jumping off the dock? You made such a big splash! I love camping!"

We went camping for a week and had so much fun. At night it was dark and a little scary. Luckily, the stars shone brightly most nights. Sometimes the moon played peak-a-boo too!

"Mommy, remember the time Bobby and I went for a walk on the trail, and we got lost for a little bit?" I asked. "Well, it seemed like forever. We kept turning the wrong way and nothing looked familiar. All the trees looked the same. We were so scared. But then you heard our voices and found us. I promise we won't do that again!"

"Yes, your Daddy and I will never forget that," she said. "We were so worried we wouldn't find you. That experience taught you and Bobby not to wander away by yourselves, didn't it? You really scared us. The bush is so big. You need to stay close to adults when camping."

Family time, campfires, and marshmallows were the best. By the time we crawled into our tent at night, it didn't take long for us all to fall asleep. Fresh air, crickets chirping, frogs croaking, loons singing, and the crackling of the campfire added to our camping memories. We always looked forward to going camping and getting back home too. Vacations were amazing.

"Olivia, Mommy isn't feeling well," Daddy said one day. "She is going to stay home from work today."

"Why?" I asked.

"She has been getting headaches and the doctor told her to rest for a few days, maybe the whole week. Resting will help Mommy feel better, so please try to help when you can. You and Bobby are such good helpers. Perhaps you can take her some juice and sit with her to keep her company? If she is sleeping, you could just sit quietly with her too. Having you near will make her feel better, I'm sure. If you think Mommy needs something, call me or Grandma right away. And don't worry, when you are at school Grandma is going to come and stay with Mommy. She'll help make meals and do whatever else she can," Daddy explained.

"Yes, Daddy. I can help," I told him. "I can set the table, put groceries away, fold laundry, and take out the garbage. Bobby and I can take turns sitting with Mommy too. Can I pick her some flowers? Maybe that would make her feel better? But Daddy, I am worried about Mommy. Will she be okay? When does she have to go back to the doctor?" I asked.

"Well, Olivia," Daddy said. "We'll see how Mommy is feeling in a week, to see if she needs to go back. Mommy would be very proud of you offering to help. I know you are trying to be very brave. Know that Daddy and Mommy love you very much."

But Mommy didn't get better. "Olivia, Mommy's headaches aren't getting better so the doctor wants Mommy to go to the hospital for some tests. The doctor needs to figure out what is causing her headaches. While Mommy is in the hospital, Grandma will help us and will be here when you and Bobby get off the bus. I know you are both scared—we are all worried about Mommy—but try not to worry too much.

We are a family, and we help each other however we can. Being brave is a big help for everyone. Know that you can always talk to Daddy or your grandparents. Hugs and talking help all of us feel a little better. Being quiet is okay too. We all need our own time in our rooms.

The important thing is that Mommy is in the best place for the doctor to find out what is wrong. Hopefully the medicine the doctor gives her helps Mommy to come home soon."

I tried to be brave but started to cry. "Daddy, can we go see Mommy? Or call her on the telephone? I miss her so much."

"I don't want to go to school," I told Daddy. "I can't think about anything else. I want to stay home. When will Mommy be home?"

Daddy didn't look happy but tried to reason with me. "Olivia, it is better to go to school. Keeping busy will help. We all want Mommy here, but she has to feel better first. We will see about visiting or calling her."

Mommy did come home a few days later, but her face was really white. I could tell she didn't feel well. "Mommy I'm so glad you are home," I cried as I gave her a hug. "We just want you to get better. Bobby and I will help Daddy and be with you when we can."

The next day, Grandma met us at the bus stop. I knew something was wrong. "Grandma, is it Mommy?" I asked.

"Dear, your Daddy needs to talk to you and your brother." When we got home, Daddy took me for a walk.

"Olivia, Mommy had to go back to the hospital as her headaches are worse. She is in a lot of pain. When I get to the hospital, I will let you and Bobby know how she is doing. We could use a miracle right now."

"Daddy," I cried. "I asked for a miracle to make Mommy better. Why isn't it working? Miracles are supposed to work. Please tell the doctor to make her better. I want to believe in miracles. Why is it taking so long?"

But Mommy didn't come home from the hospital. "I'm not sure how to tell you this," said Daddy when he came home alone, "but Mommy died today. The doctor couldn't do anything more for Mommy. He tried so hard to make her better."

Bobby and I didn't even get to see her or give her a hug and tell her we loved her. Daddy cried and we cried. Tears came hard for many hours. Everyone was crying in disbelief.

"I know you are extremely upset and can't understand what has happened. I am sad and confused too. There are lots of things to talk about, but for right now let's hug each other and know that Mommy's love will be in our hearts forever." Daddy whispered.

Daddy told us that Mommy became an angel after she died.

"Mommy...where are you? Why aren't you coming home? Daddy! This can't be happening! I don't believe you. This can't be true. This is just a bad dream...she is going to come back."

Mommy, I still have so much to learn. Every day, you taught me something. I'm so confused now. You were always here for me. I miss the warmth in your hugs and your strength. You made me laugh. You wiped my tears. You have seen me troubled. You have seen and made me happy. I'm really scared and so, so sad. I feel like I'm in the dark and no one cares about me or how I feel.

Mommies don't die! They are supposed to be here forever! Who is going to love me? Who is going to talk to me? Who will tuck me into bed? Who is going to love me like you did? How do we live without you? I want you to kiss me goodnight. You always kissed me goodnight. You said to be strong…I am trying, but it feels impossible. My heart hurts. I needed more time with you. You weren't supposed to die. You were my everything. What am I to do now? Your chair is empty. The house feels empty. My heart is empty, and I hurt inside. I can't stop crying.

Daddy said that Heaven was a place up in the clouds. He thought that angels were in the stars where they are watching and protecting us from Heaven. He said that Mommy's soul is inside my heart and the love will always be there to comfort me. Mommy will be an angel in a star just for us. I don't understand. I need to be stronger to try to understand.

One night I went outside to look at the stars, just to see if I could find you.
I can't believe that you died. What if we lose Daddy too? Which star are you, Mommy? How can you protect me when you are in heaven? Where do angels sleep?
How do they get in the stars?

It took me a long time to accept that maybe Mommy could be an angel, but she was gone. Each morning, I woke up thinking she would be there. Sitting at the table or on the couch. But she wasn't. Angels are special. She would make a beautiful angel!

"Olivia, I know you have so many questions," Daddy said. "I'll try to explain and give you some answers, but you might not understand everything until you are a little older. Adults don't understand everything, and we don't have all the answers either. This is hard for everyone. Mommy was very sick. Her headaches caused problems that the doctor couldn't fix. Mommy's heart stopped. That means she couldn't breathe or move anymore. Her body just wouldn't work right to keep her alive. Sometimes doctors can't save everyone. Sometimes miracles work in ways we don't understand. Talking about Mommy will help all of us.

We have to plan a tribute in Mommy's honour. A tribute to the person who died is called a funeral. A funeral is where Mommy's body will be placed for family and friends to say goodbye. I will be there to help you through the next few days as we plan Mommy's funeral and how we will say goodbye to Mommy," Daddy explained through his tears.

"Perhaps you and Bobby could draw Mommy a picture and put one of your teddy bears with her for the funeral? Saying goodbye is really hard, but it is important. Your picture and teddy would make Mommy happy that you shared those things with her. You are going to feel sad and upset for some time. That is normal when you lose someone. Being scared is normal too. You don't have to be brave all the time. Remember that Daddy and your grandparents are here to talk to whenever you want. If you want to be by yourself, that's okay too."

"Mommy was a good person and loved us, so why did she have to die?" I asked Daddy.

"She didn't want to die sweetheart," Daddy said. "The doctor couldn't help her. We can't bring her back as much as we all want her to be here. She will be watching you and cheering you on in different ways. Mommy will want you to find your smile again and find the courage to feel like yourself again. Happiness can only start with you. Mommy will want you to continue playing, going to school, and having fun. We all love you and you are safe. The sadness and loss you are feeling is called grief. These are your emotions. Finding a way to heal your broken heart is about finding things that help you. Everyone handles grief and sadness differently, but you need to understand that Mommy will always be in your heart.

You may need to cry, scream, be afraid, angry, or sad. Then you need to be still, breathe, and find yourself so you're maybe not as scared. Trying to heal your heart will be your own journey. You have lots of memories with Mommy. We went camping, picked strawberries, played, and worked together. Those memories and feelings will never go away," Daddy explained.

"Olivia, remember her voice, her touch, her smile, and her love. There will be new little signs you might see, or feel, or think you see or feel. You know how she liked dragonflies, cardinals, and butterflies? Maybe Mommy's favourite things will show up. You can talk to Mommy still. Please know that you are not alone. Pretending you are okay only works for a time. But you need to find strength within you to live without Mommy here."

"When will I feel okay again?" I whispered. "One day she is here and the next she is gone. Do you think she knew she was going to die? We didn't get enough days with her, Daddy."

"Someday you will understand, but right now we have to help each other. You need to trust me that you will feel differently in time. There will be lots of questions and some I might not be able to answer for you. I miss Mommy every day too. We all do. We will all have different feelings or emotions on different days. Our family has to stay strong together to work through our own grief," Daddy shared.

"Daddy, I love you. But I really miss Mommy, and I feel angry. I do have many different feelings, you are right. I need Mommy. My heart feels so heavy.
I wish we could change things."

Is this just a dream? It can't be true…that you are gone forever? Mommy, I miss you so much. I feel so lonely. Daddy says that things will get better. I wish I could talk to you in person. Daddy said that he was here and would keep me safe. Everyone is trying to cheer me up. Sometimes I just want to be by myself and then other times I want to be around others. I think about you every day, Mommy. We can't always have what we want. I asked for a miracle, but it didn't work. But it isn't a dream…is it?

Then one day I realized…

I need to honour you Mommy. I have to get up every day without you. To honour you, I have to take little steps, one at a time. To honour you, I need to trust that I will be okay. To honour you, I will always remember your smile, your laugh, your eyes, and your love. To honour you, you will be alive in my heart forever. I am a good person, and I have the courage to do this! I need to love myself to grow. Perhaps my miracle was having you as my Mommy!

Mommy…to honour you, I need to keep going. I need to be brave and strong just like you told me. I need to keep dreaming and never give up. Sometimes being strong isn't enough, and it's okay to ask for help. Sometimes I can be brave but if I'm not, I know that's okay too. I can't change what has happened–I have to accept you are gone. It is time to discover the world around me. I am grateful for each new day. I have to hold my head up high like you would want me to. I want to make you proud of me, Mommy.

If I listen hard and watch for signs, maybe I will hear a sound, your laugh, your voice, or a song you loved. Maybe I'll feel the warmth of your touch from the sunshine. Maybe I'll smell something like your perfume. I might see a butterfly, dragonfly, or cardinal, or a look that reminds me of your smile. Your hugs and your goodnight kisses are things that make me smile and sad at the same time. Your strength has made me grateful for each day and helps me to believe in myself.

Friends say I've changed a lot, I said a lot changed me. My Mom was the most beautiful Mom in the world. I will love you forever, Mom! Memories of you will be with me for life. Thank you for your kisses each night. I am who I am because of you.

Treasure the memories.
Cherish the love.
Always kiss me goodnight.

About the Author

I am a mother, wife, grandmother, relative, and friend to many, and I am so grateful for each day. My six grandchildren call me Grandma or "Dee Dee" and my love for them and my own grown children is unconditional. Waking up each day is a miracle that sometimes we take for granted. I feel that we are born to be someone on this earth, and my focus has been on being a good person and helping others. Life is a learning journey as are relationships. My sincere love, commitment, and compassion have been evident in the friends I have made along my journey, the outreach in the various communities in which I have lived, and my professional performance at numerous jobs.

Losing my Mom at an early age has impacted my life in so many ways. I wanted to share a resource for parents to help them should they and their children face a tragedy like the loss of a spouse, grandparent, or friend, to help explain loss to their children. I hope that this children's book can be of some service. May you enjoy "Always Kiss Me Goodnight".

I am grateful for your interest and would welcome any feedback or questions. Please visit my website at: neversaygoodbye.ca

Acknowledgements

A grieving journey is personal, and my hope and dream of sharing and publishing a message to help children, grandparents, parents, and others wouldn't have been possible without assistance. Another thank you goes to my husband, Blair, for always being supportive, encouraging, and giving me unconditional love.

I want to thank my dear friend, Lori Thompson, for her encouragement, support, and expertise while I tackled my first book. It was a dream come true with her loving assistance. This accomplishment of publishing my personal message to others in the form of a children's book is a proud moment. Thank you, Lori.

Marcia, I can't thank you enough for your professional expertise and skills with coaching, editing, and publishing my first book, "Always Kiss Me Goodnight." Your attention to detail is amazing and your consideration of my intended audience and content of my first children's book is astounding, encouraging, and appreciated.

And thank you to my grandson, Ronan, who assisted with the awesome illustrations. His artistic ability will lead him to so many possible opportunities. Thank you for sharing your talent. This has been a special memory working together, and one I will treasure forever. Thank you, Ronan.

Additional Resources

A resource guide is available online to help facilitate difficult conversations with children who have experienced loss. The resource guide includes:

- Questions that may be asked of parent with possible corresponding responses or actions,
- A page with both negative and self-talk positive words, for the child to choose how they are feeling in the moment with a corresponding positive response or activity,
- Resources for parents to refer to for themselves or services they might leverage,
- Blank pages for children to express their emotions through drawing or writing,
- Journal pages with prompts for the child to help process their feelings, and more!

Grief is never easy, and the journey is different for everyone. This book is a conversation starter but it doesn't end here.

www.ingramcontent.com/pod-product-compliance
Lightning Source LLC
Chambersburg PA
CBHW041527070526
44585CB00003B/114